Unicorn Colouring Book

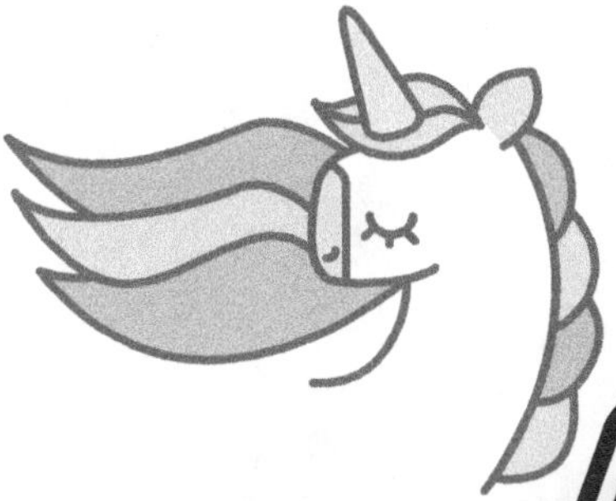

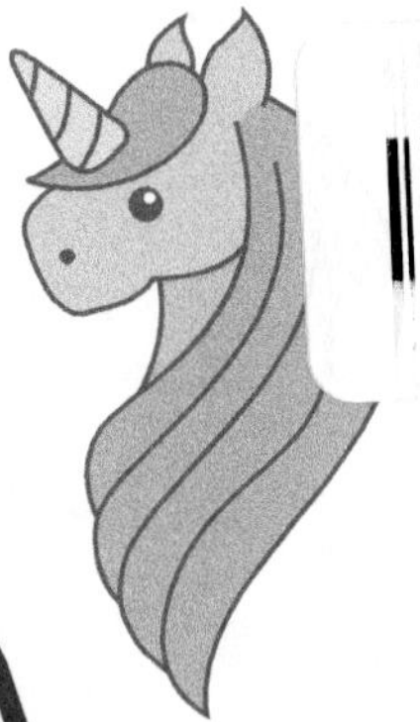

This book belongs to:

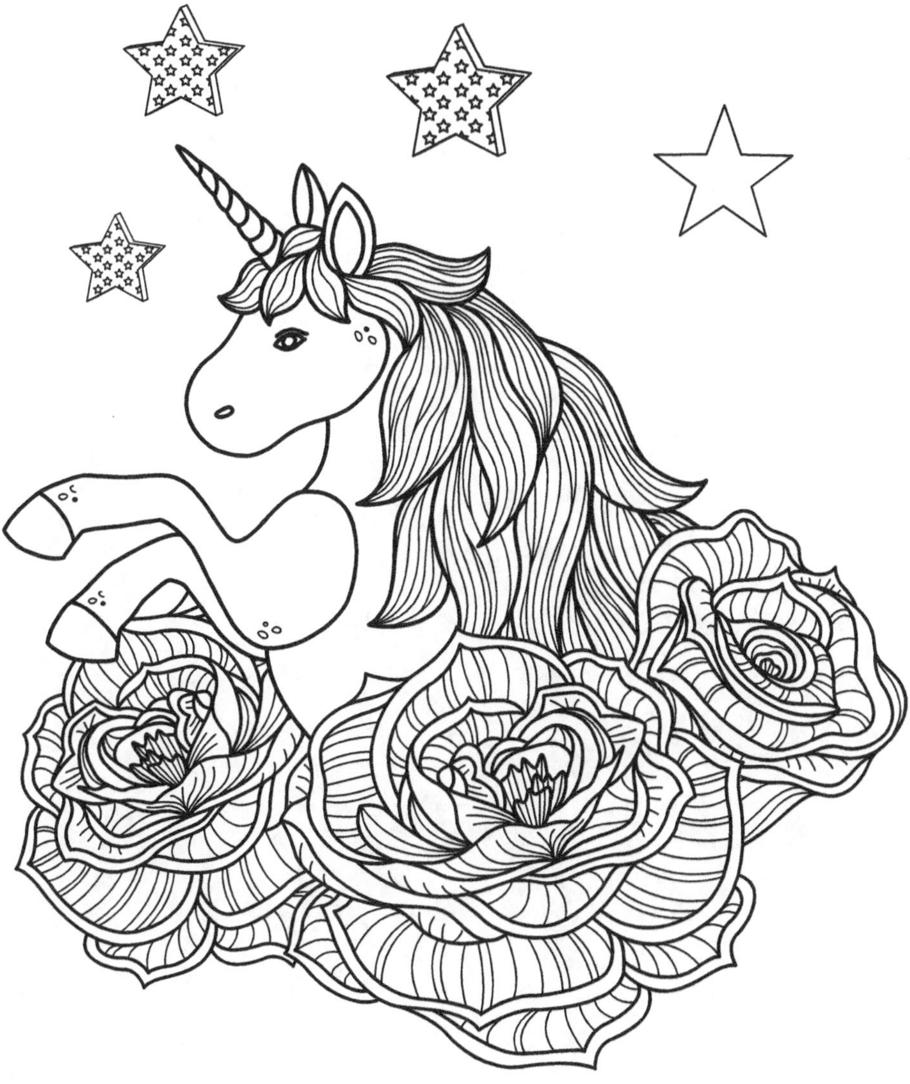

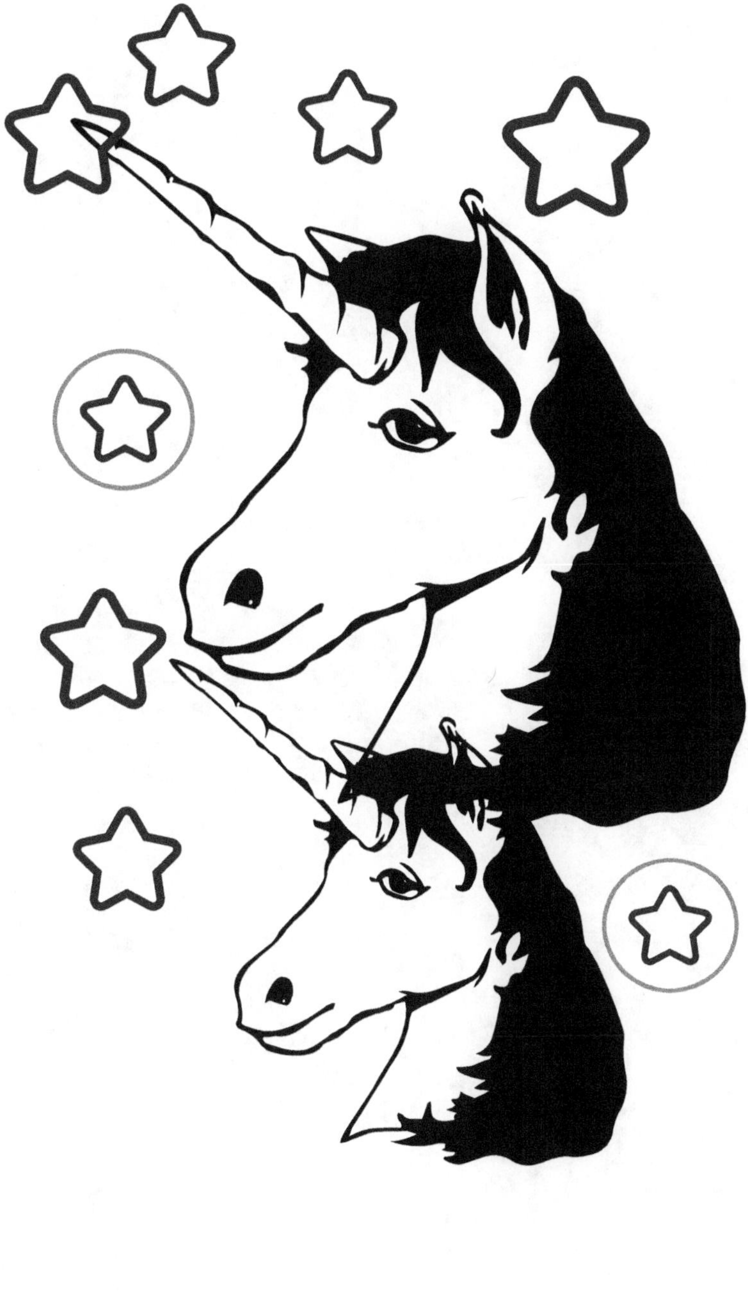

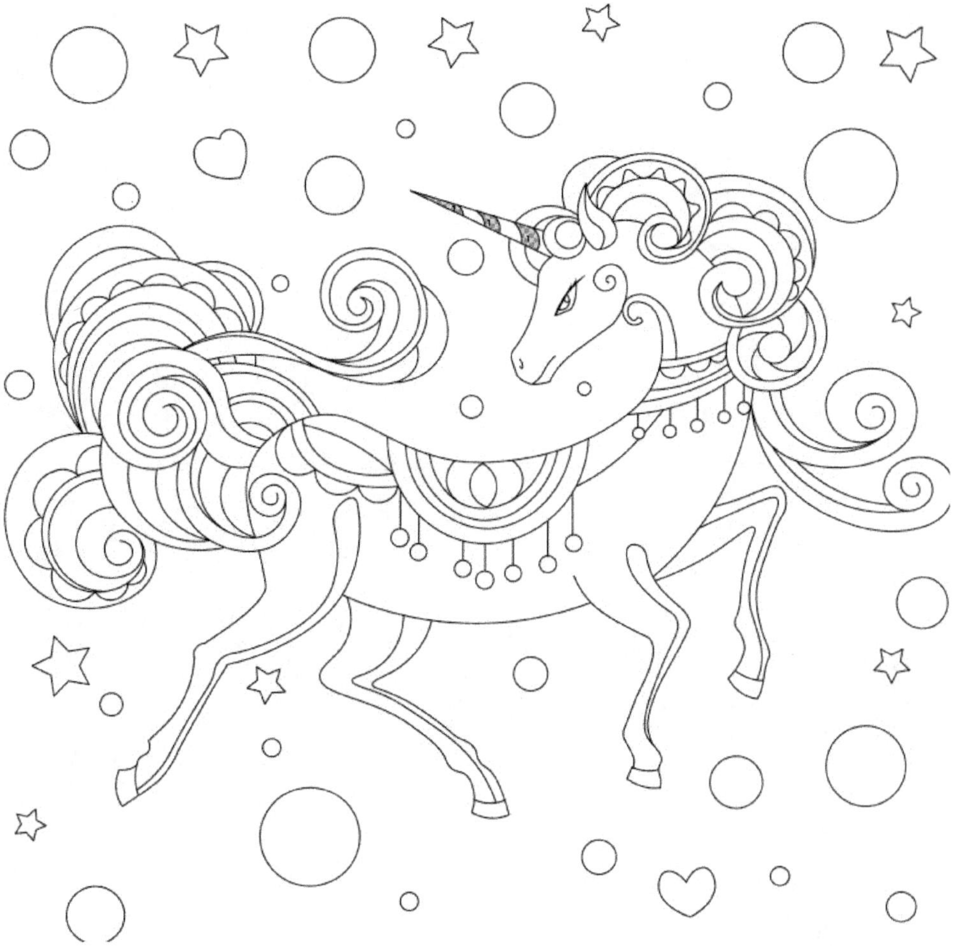

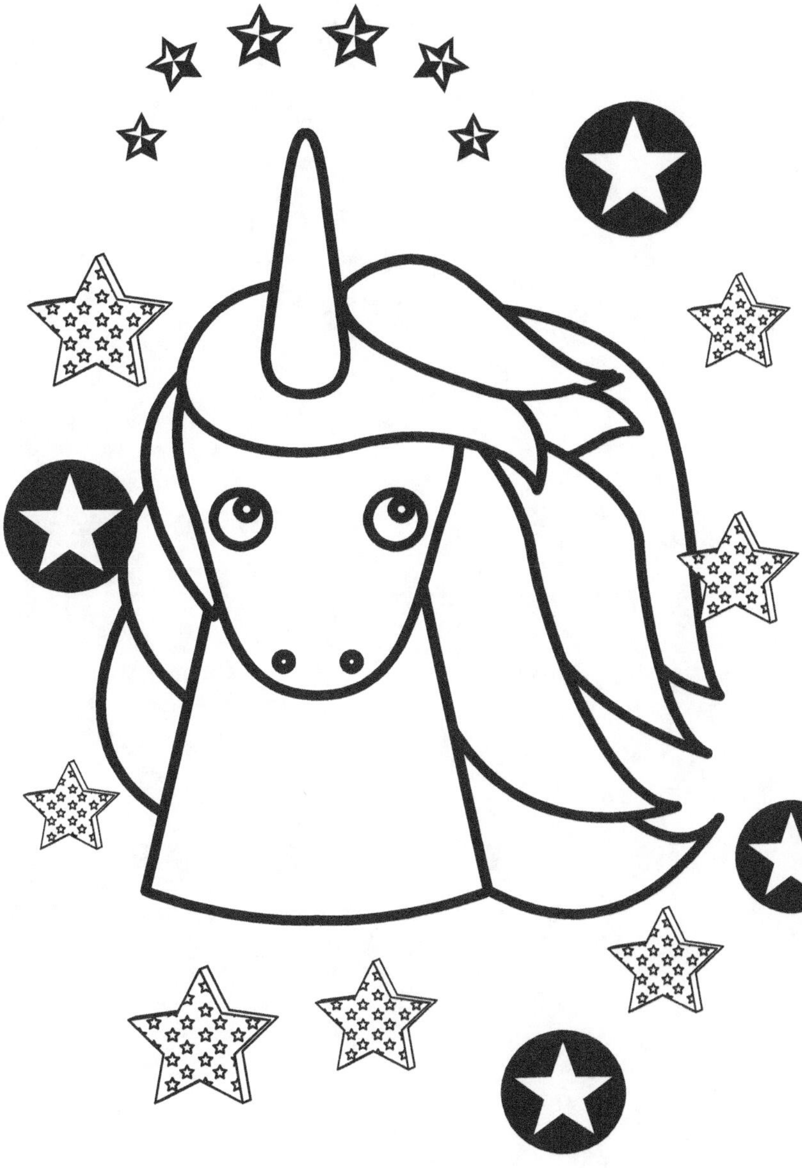

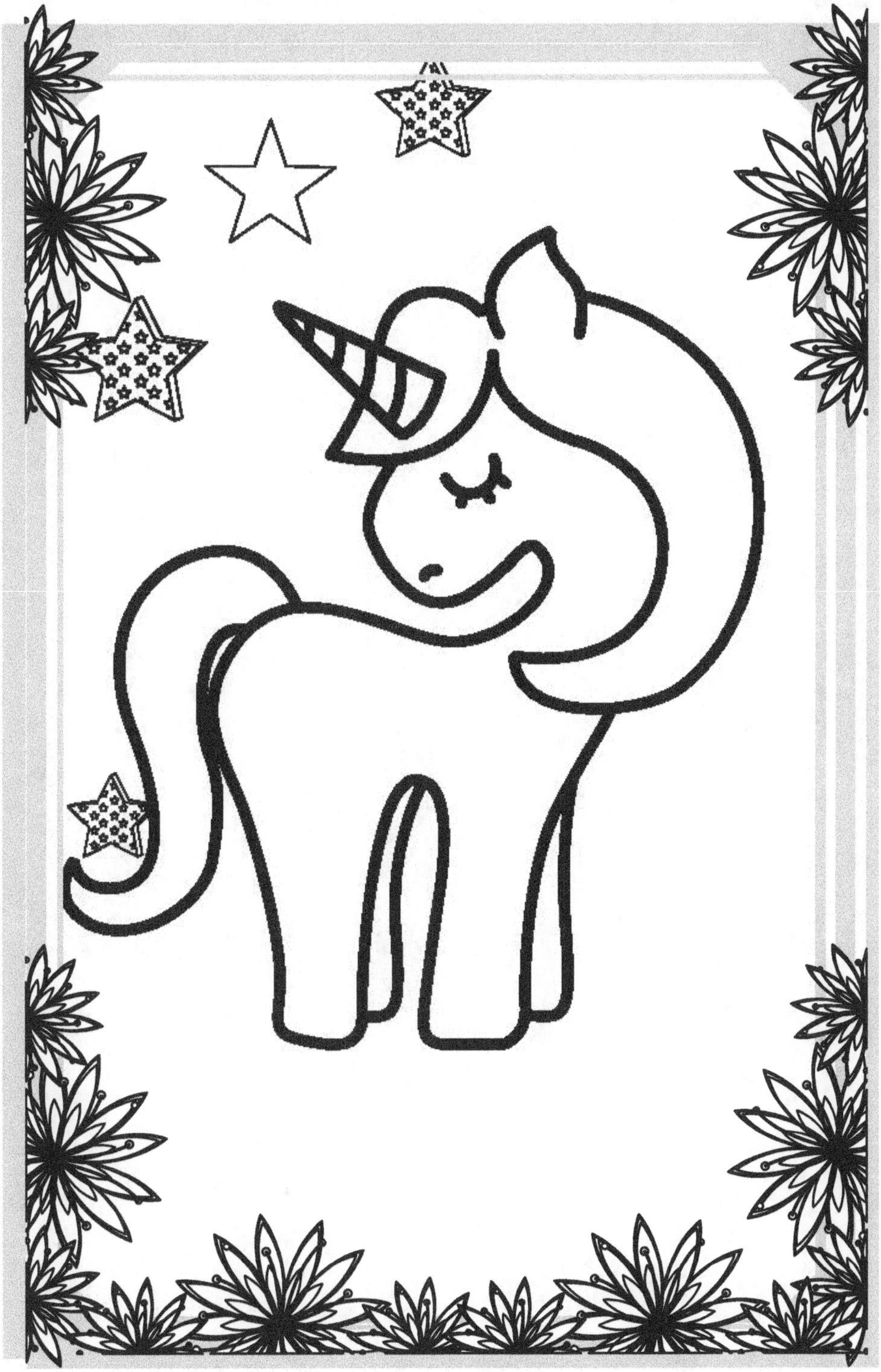

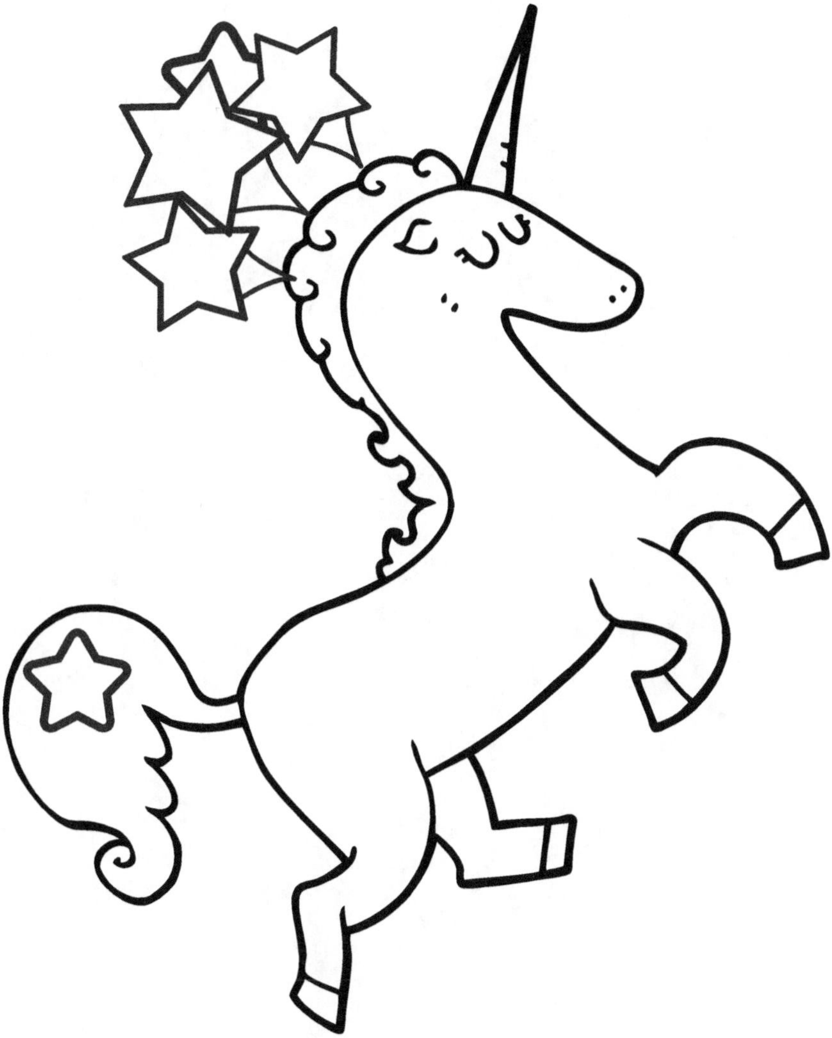

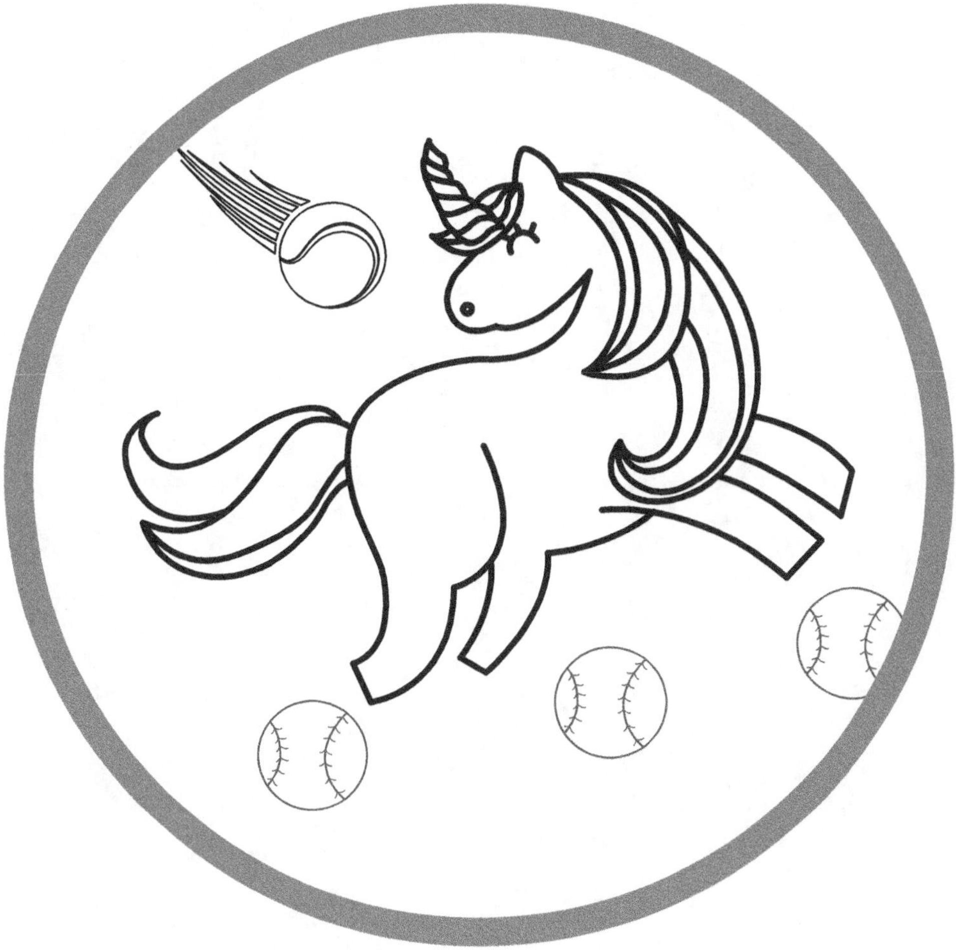

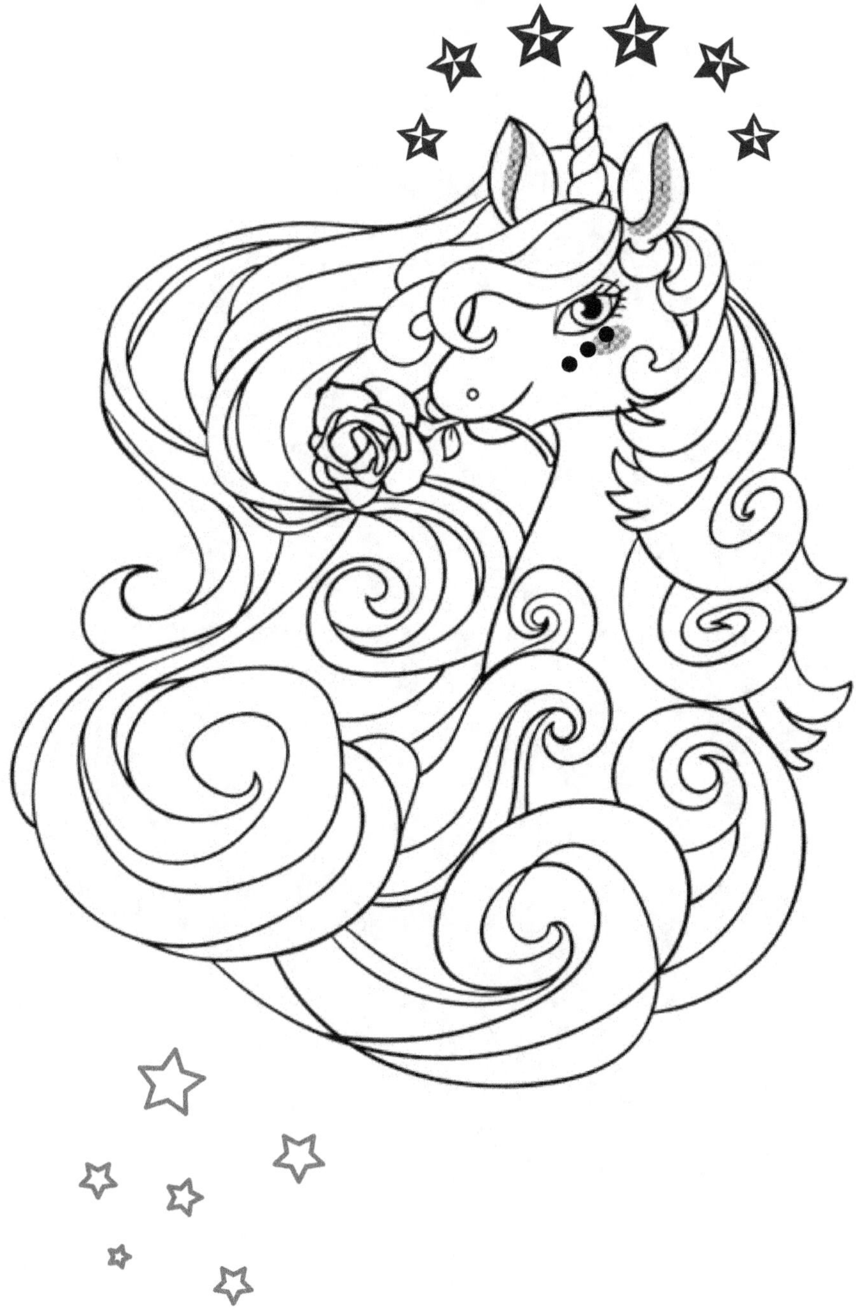

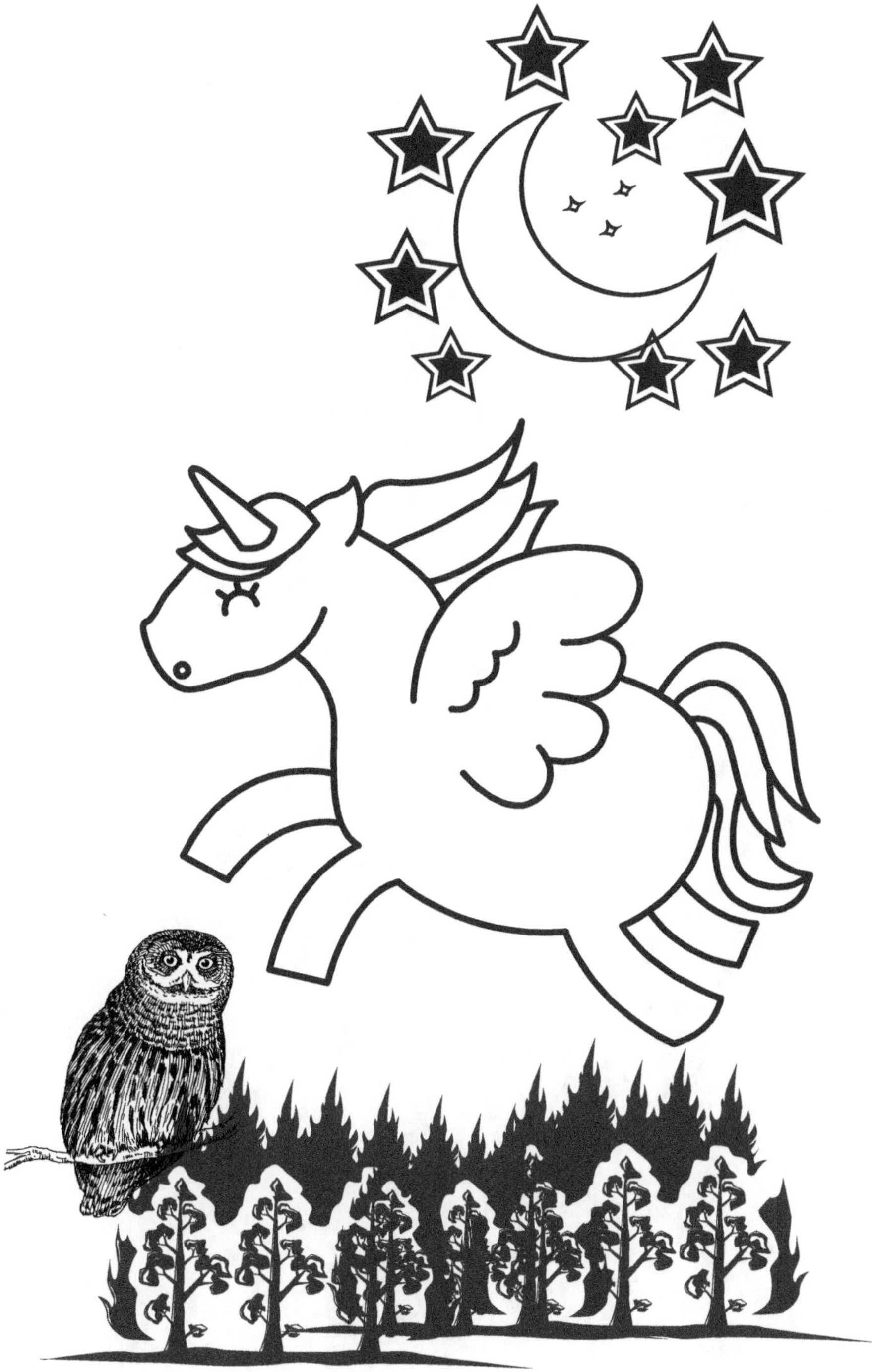

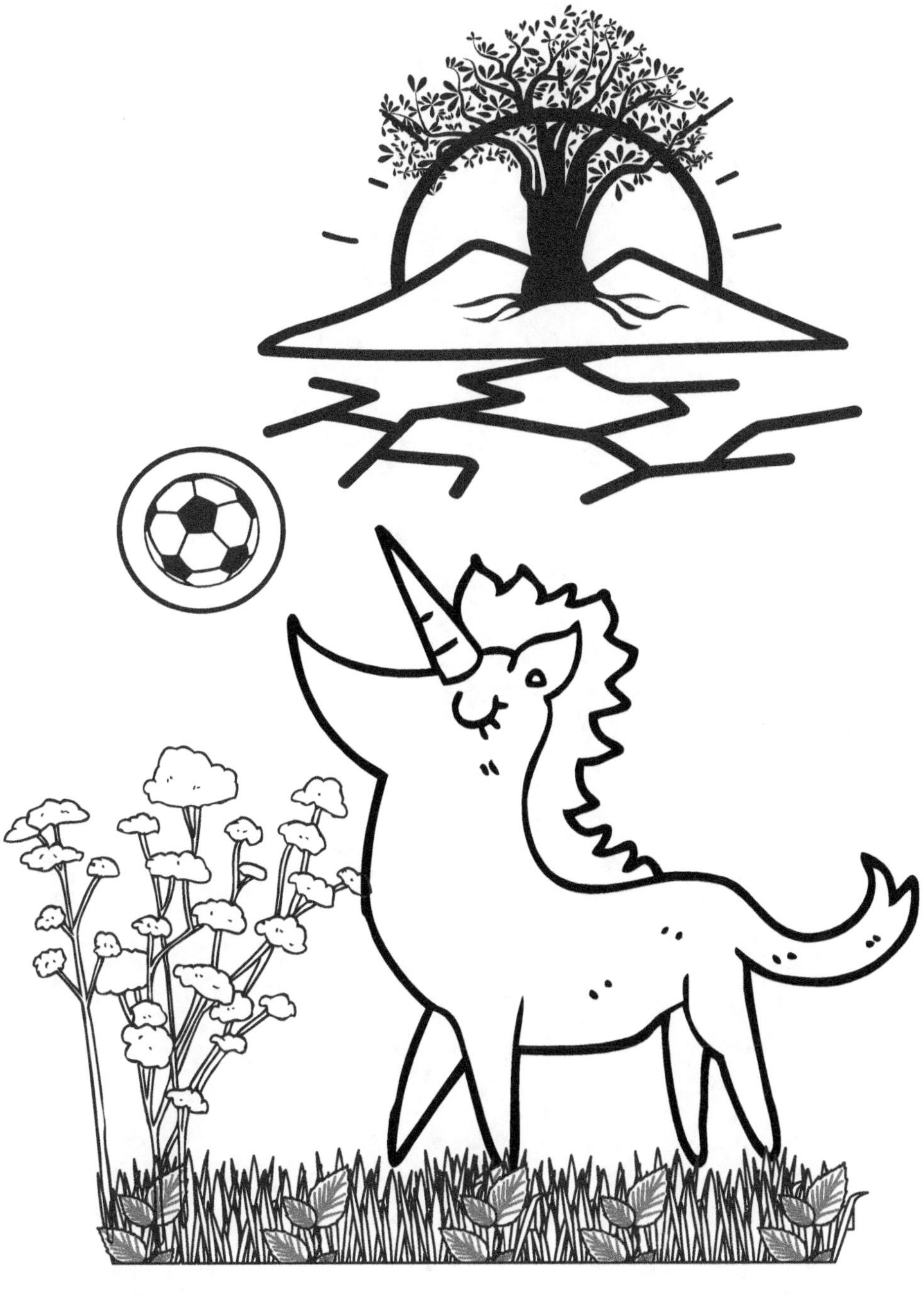

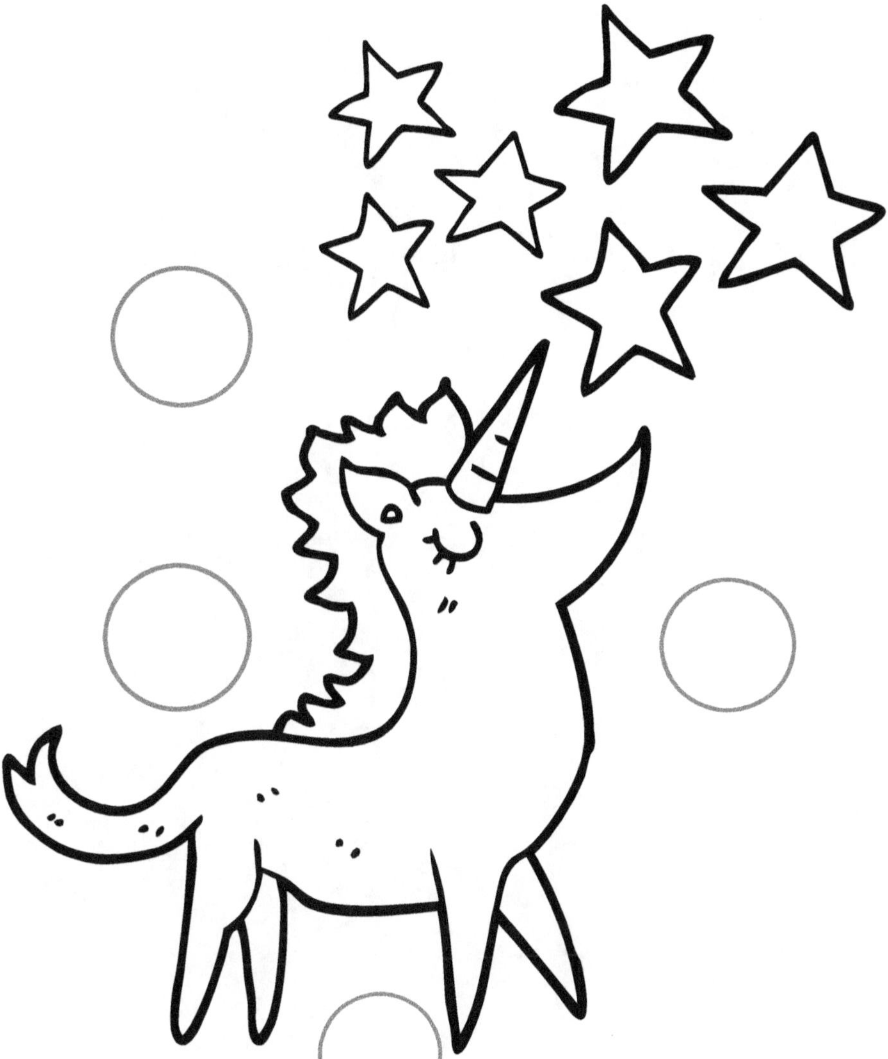

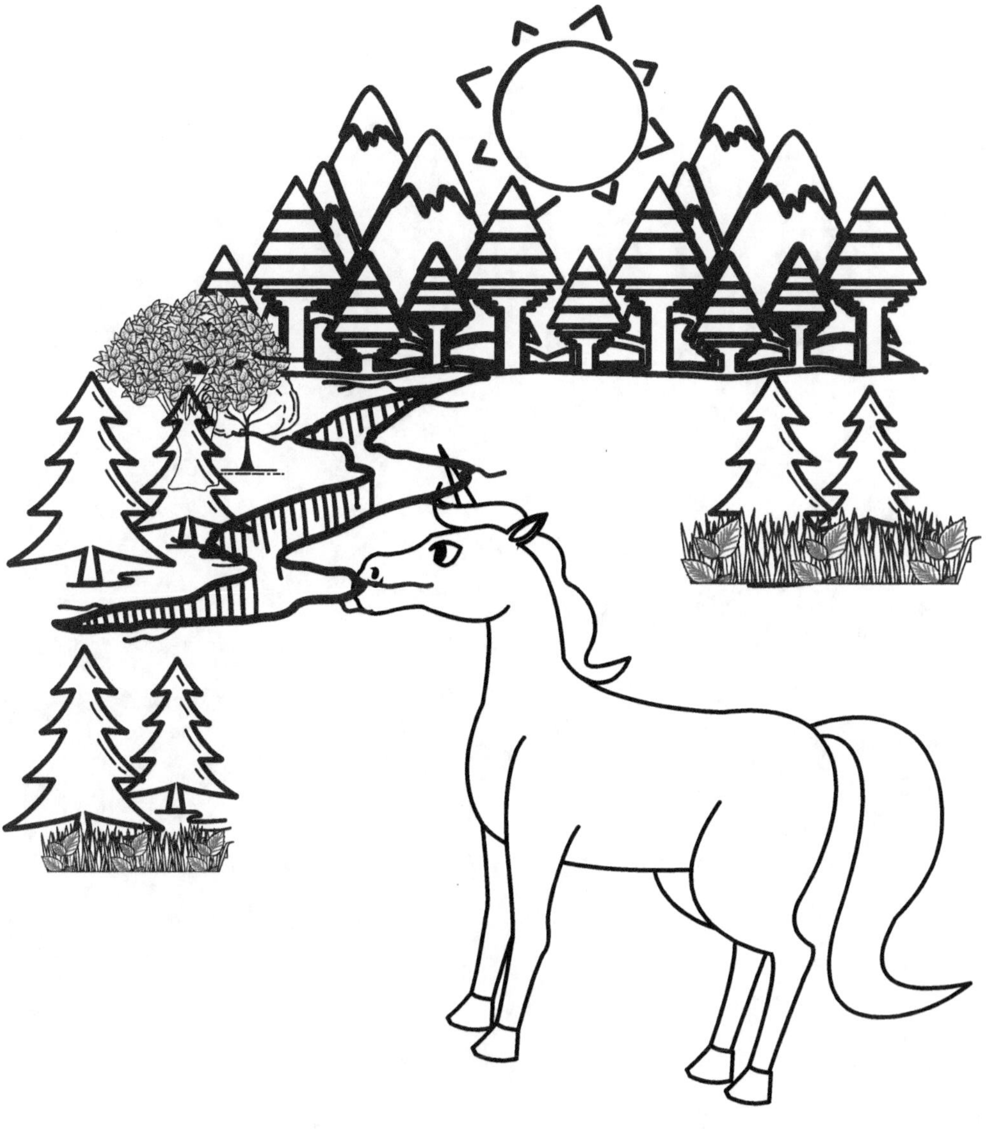

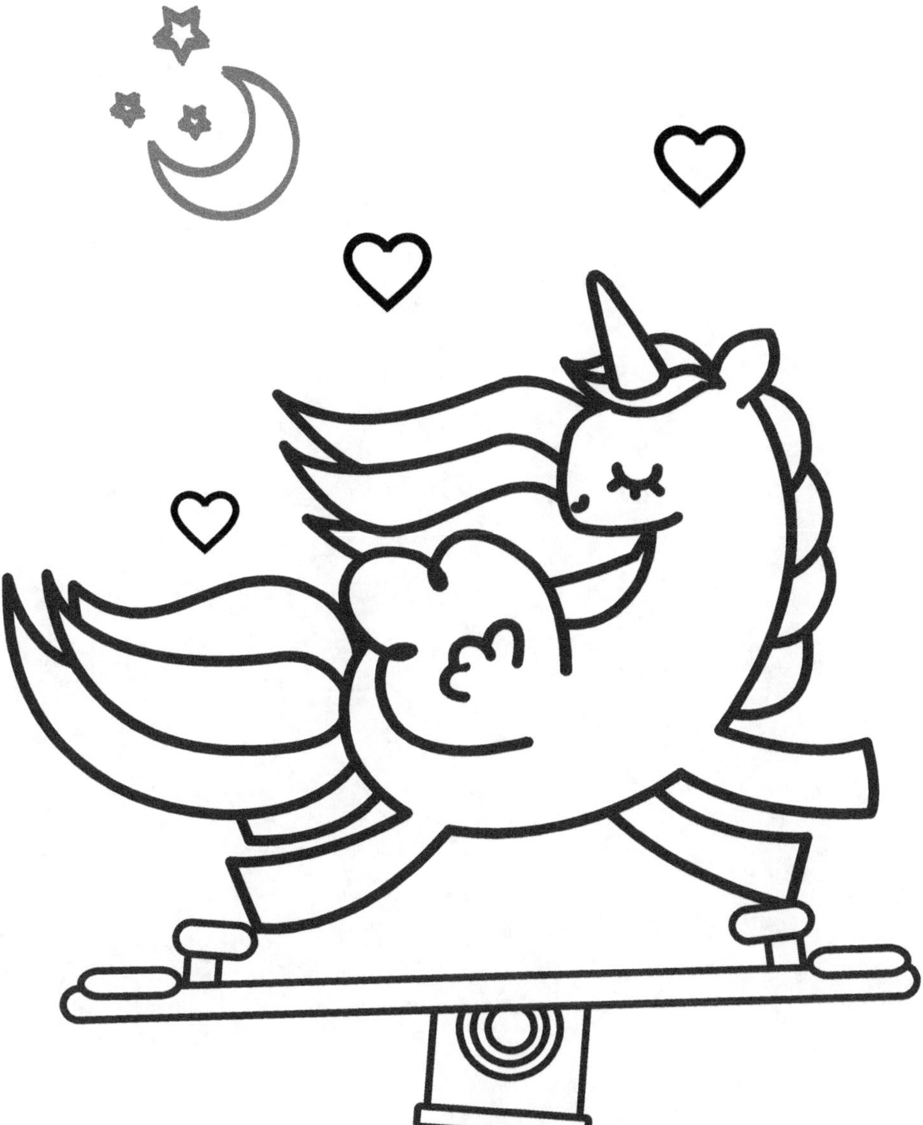

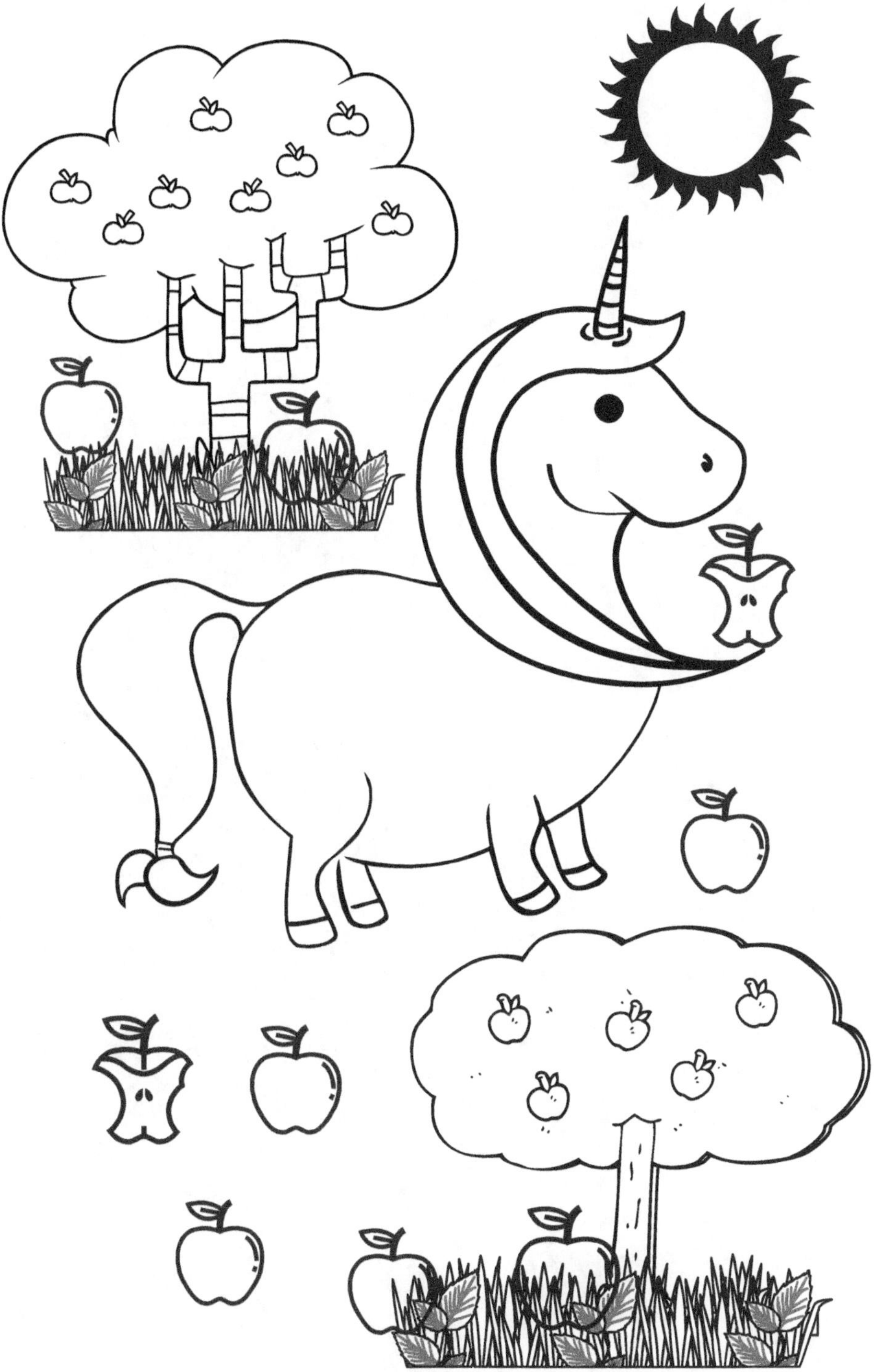

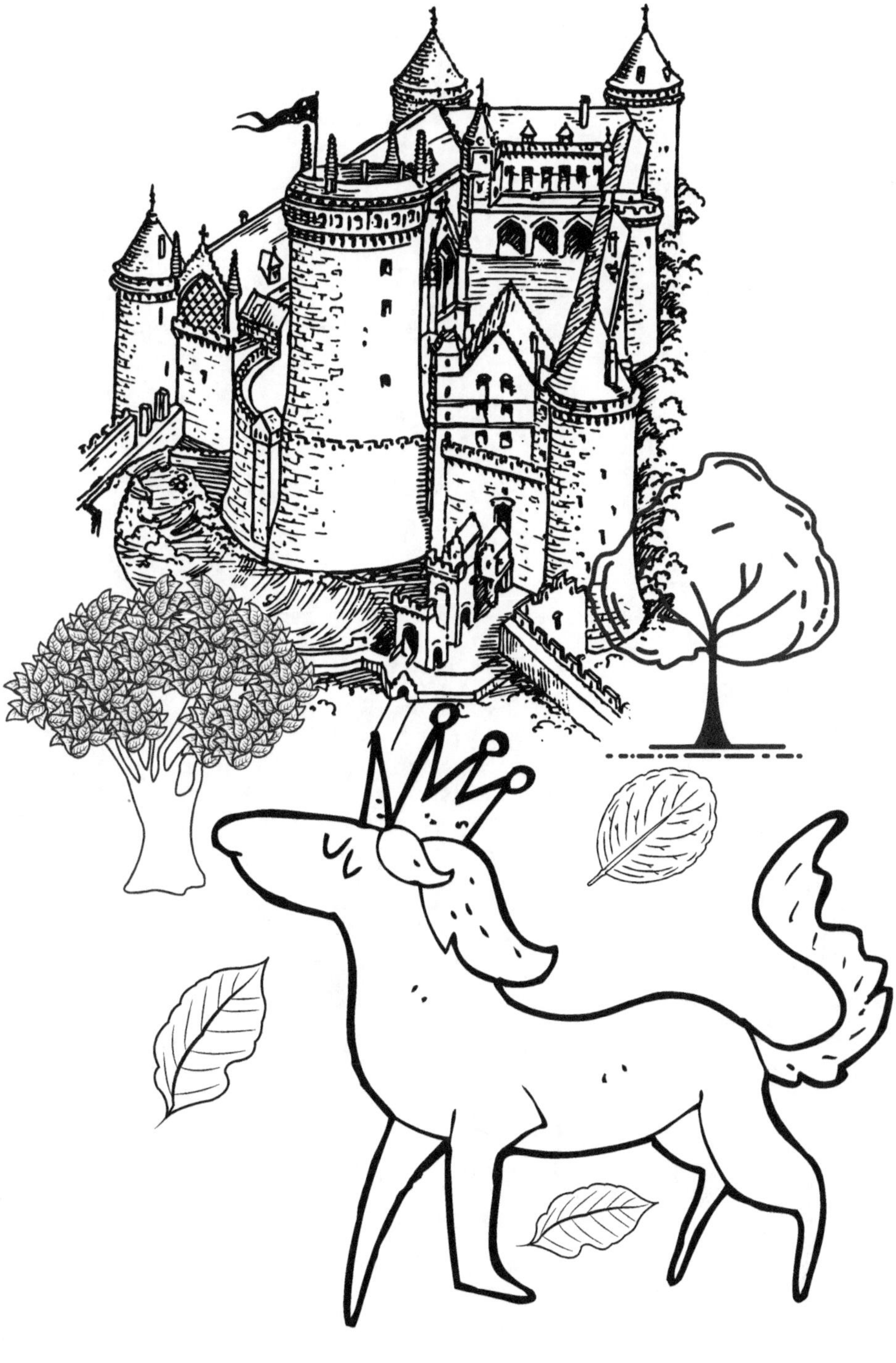

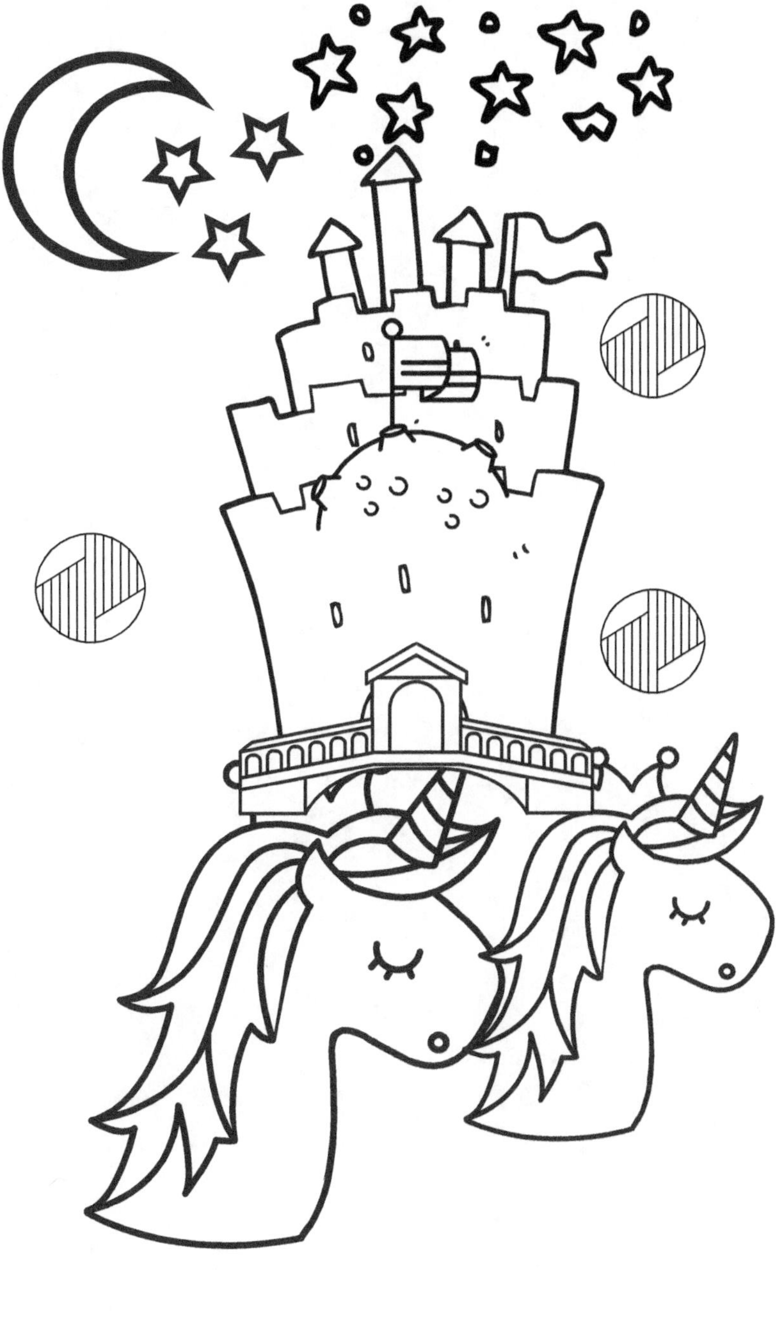

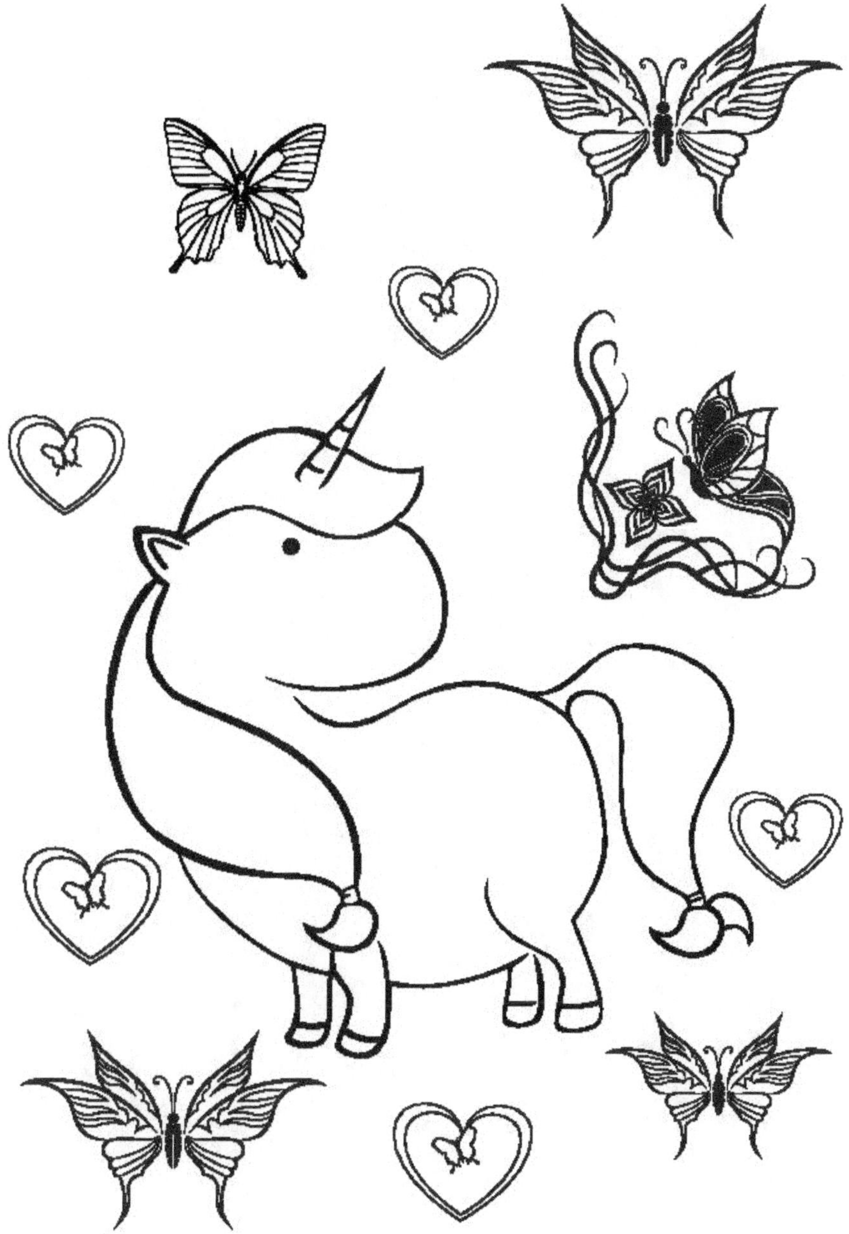

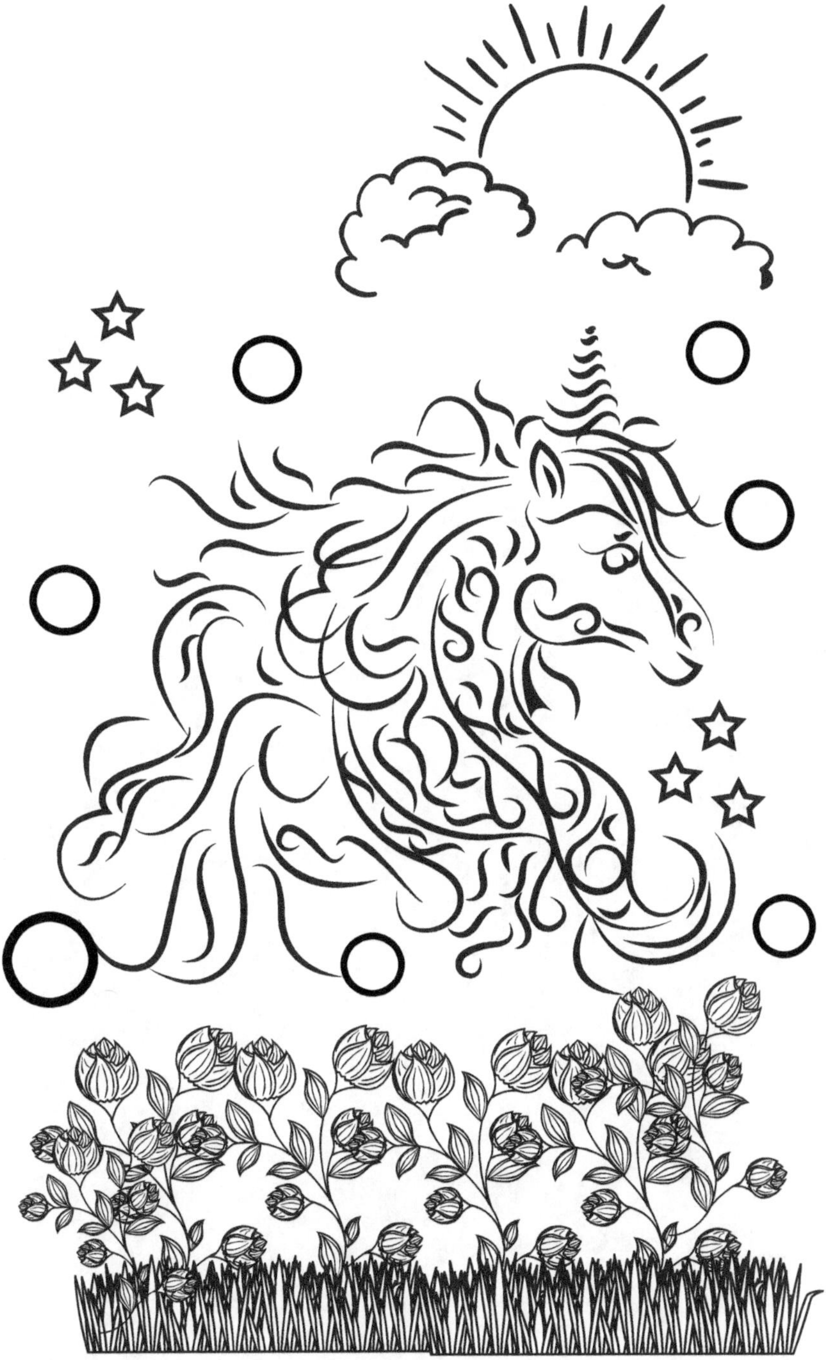

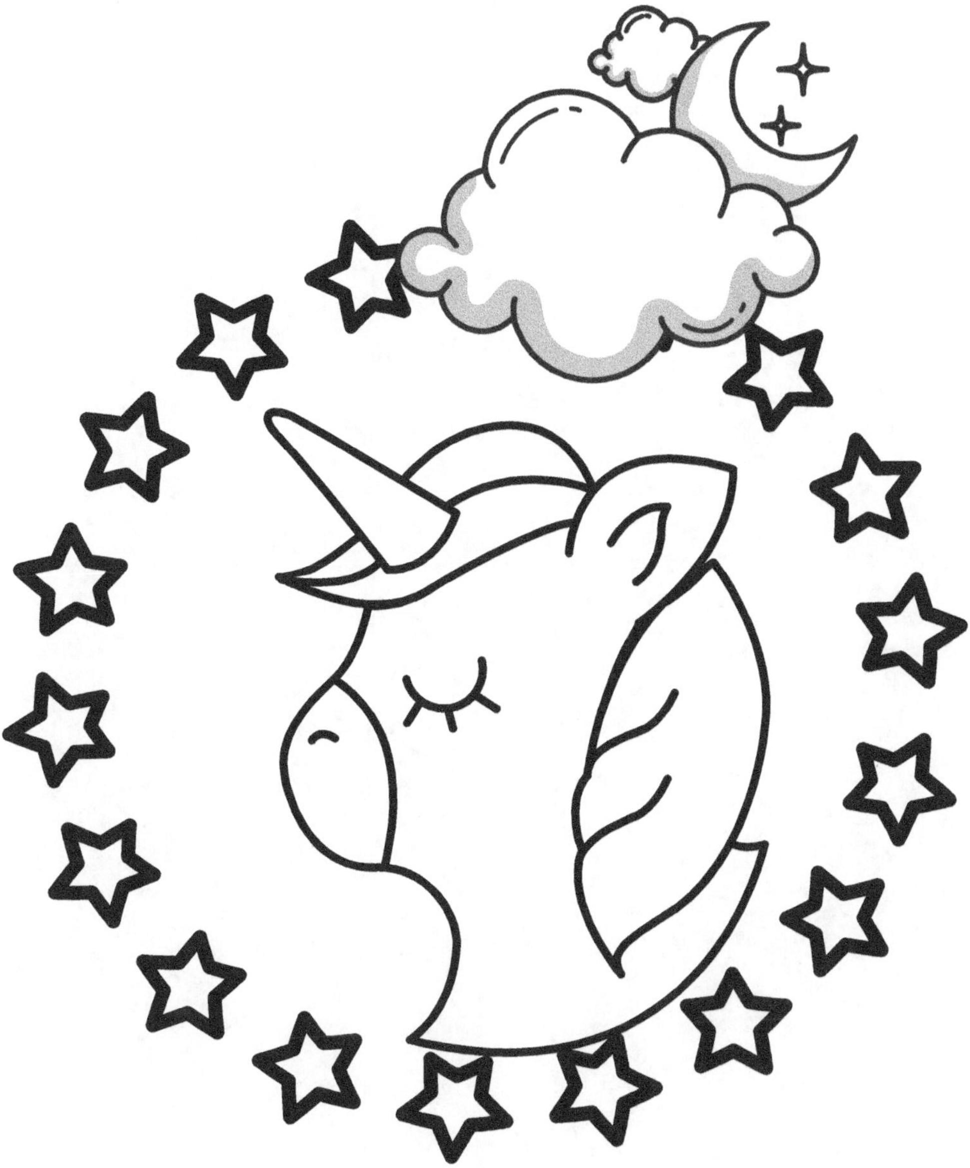

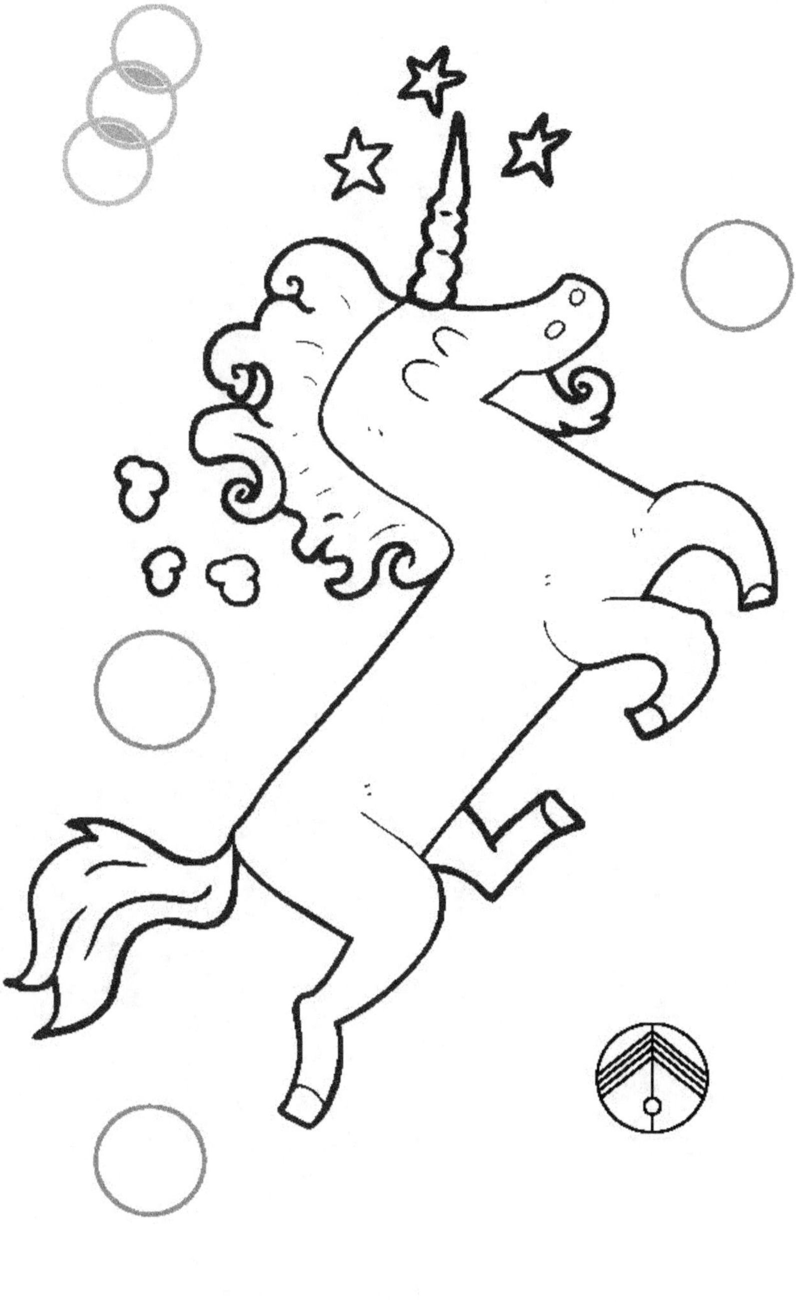

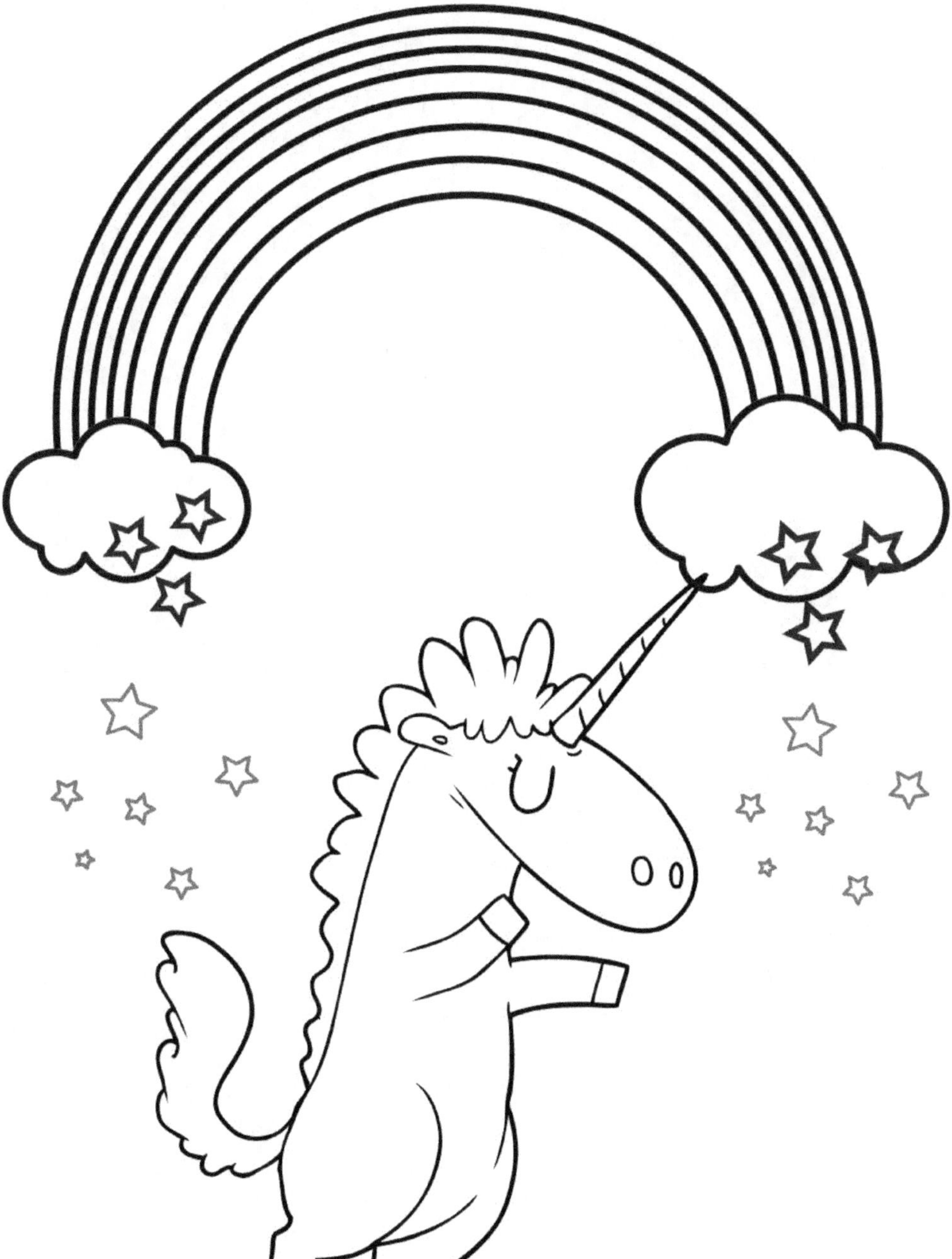

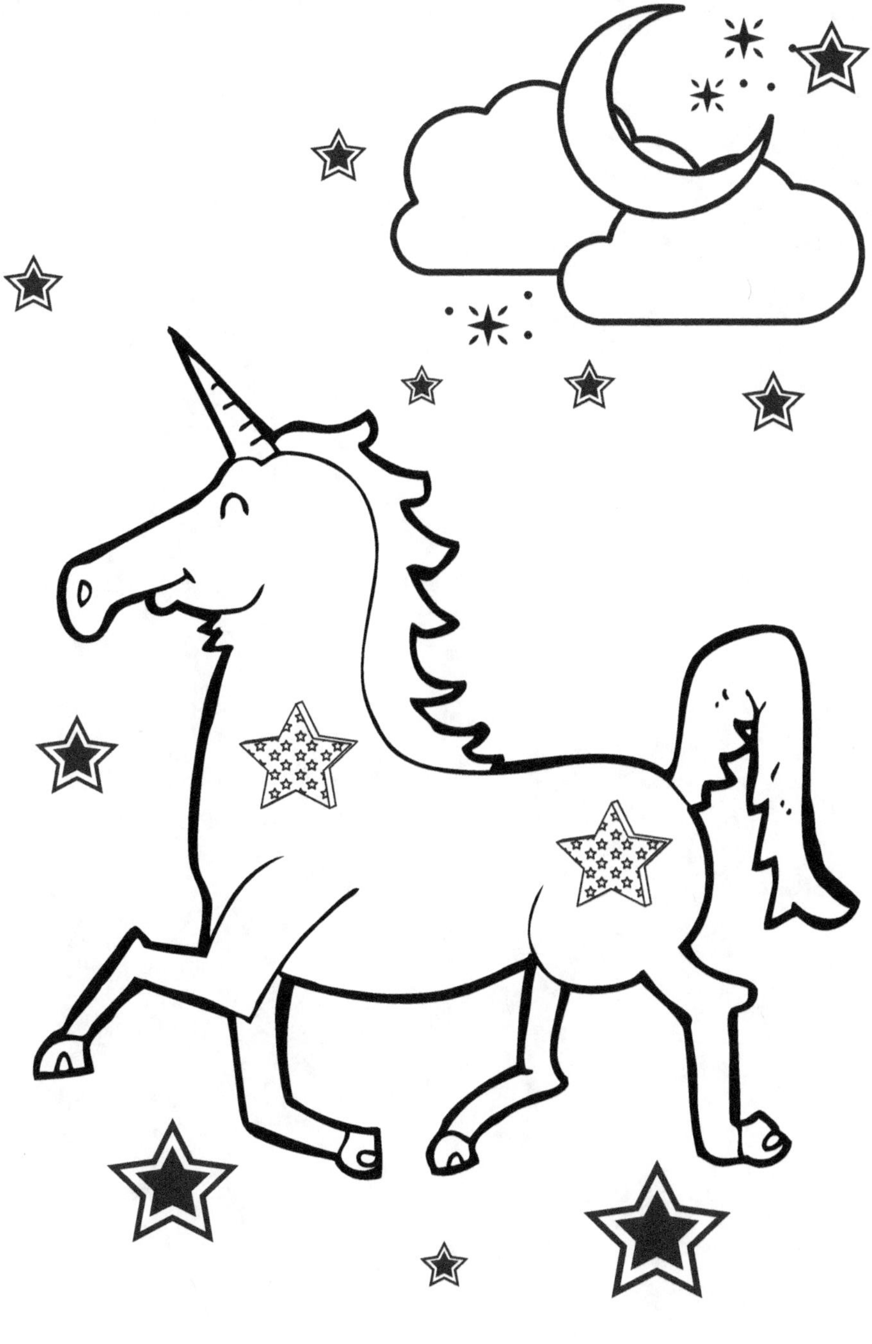

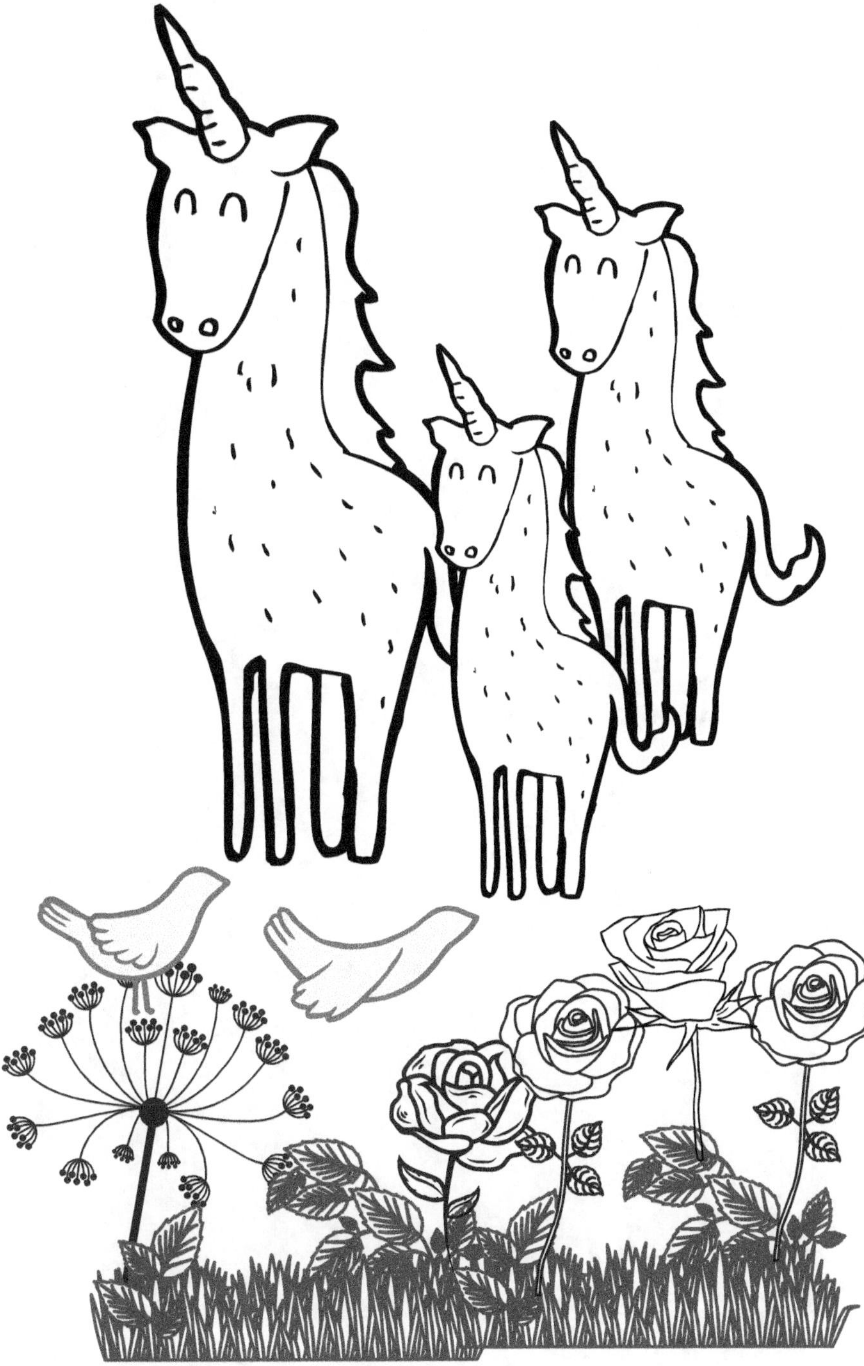

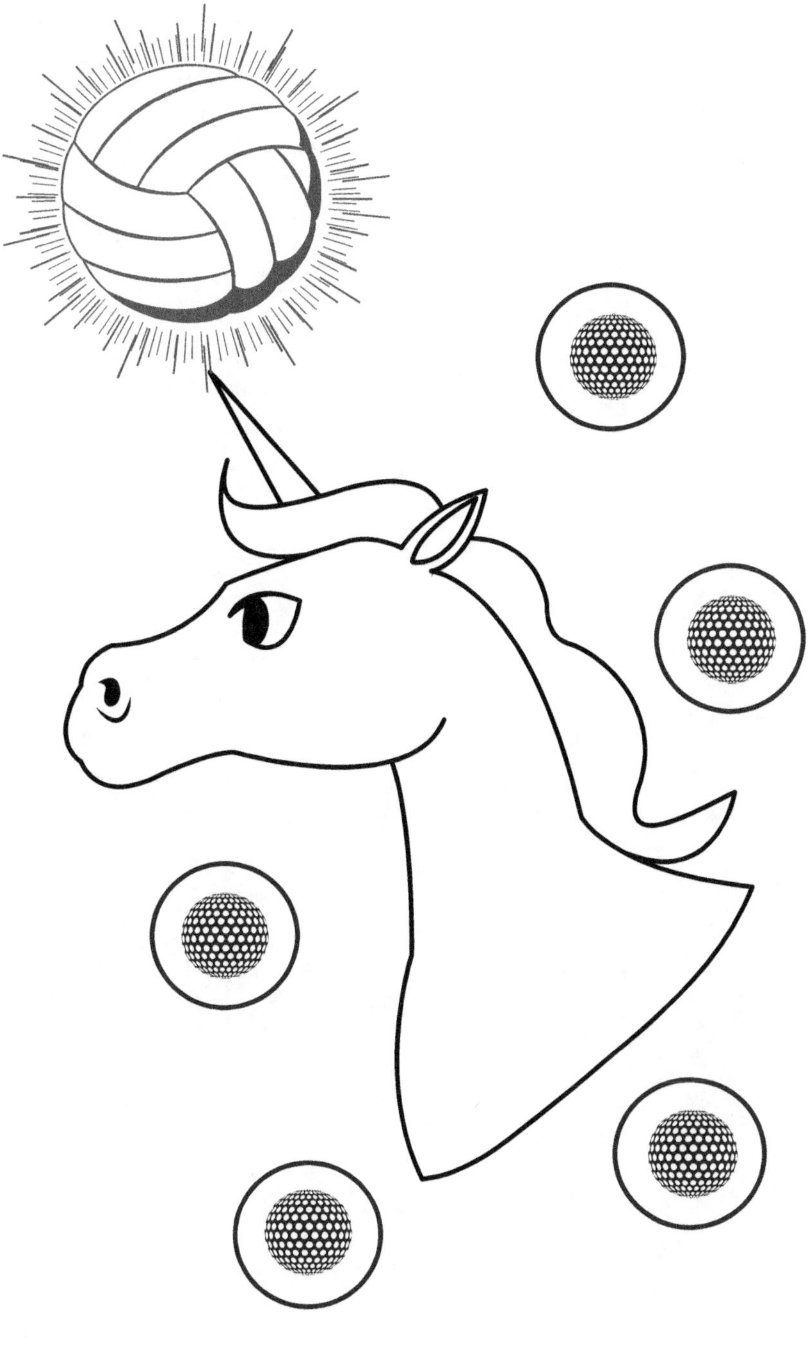

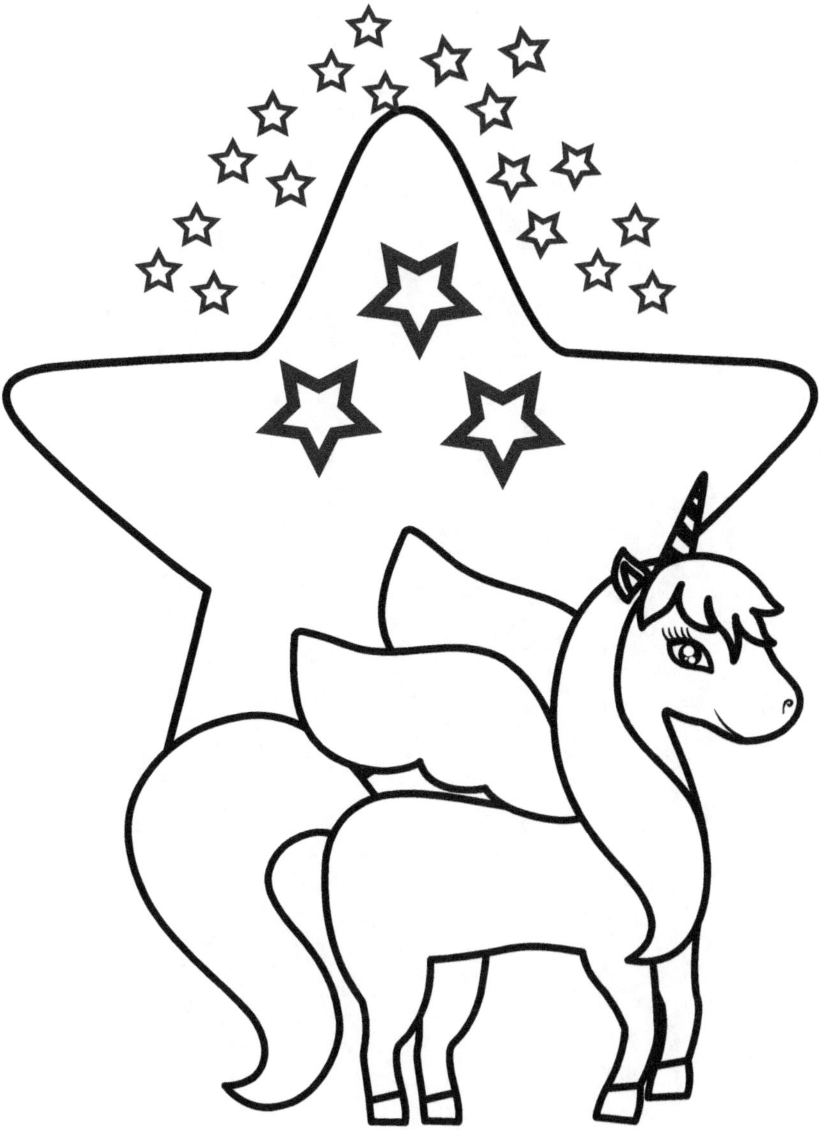

www.ingramcontent.com/pod-product-compliance
Lightning Source LLC
Chambersburg PA
CBHW050304220526
45465CB00002B/817
* 9 7 9 8 6 1 1 9 8 4 8 2 6 *